DALAI LAMA

DALAI LAMA

ODYSSEYS

MELISSA GISH

CREATIVE EDUCATION · CREATIVE PAPERBACKS

Published by Creative Education and Creative Paperbacks
P.O. Box 227, Mankato, Minnesota 56002
Creative Education and Creative Paperbacks are imprints of
The Creative Company
www.thecreativecompany.us

Design by Blue Design (www.bluedes.com)
Production by Colin O'Dea
Art direction by Rita Marshall
Printed in the United States of America

Photographs by 123rf (pat138241), Alamy (Agencja
Fotograficzna Caro, Seth K. Hughes, Prasit Rodphan, jeremy
sutton-hibbert), Bigstock (leodaphne, nopponpat, Nuttawut
Uttamaharad), Bridgeman Images (SZ Photo/Scherl), Creative
Commons Wikimedia (Sur Chakrabarty, Georg Denda/
Panoramio, Kinsey Brothers/Artribune, Homai Vyarawalla/
King's India Institute/King's College London), The Design Lab,
Getty Images (Todd Brown/The Image Bank, Chris Hondros,
Popperfoto, Alison Wright/National Geographic), iStockphoto
(AdamWong28, altmodern, Astalor, fotoVoyager, helovi,
hxdyl, Kateryna Mashkevych, skaman306, Train_Arrival, W6),
National Geographic Image Collection (ALISON WRIGHT)

Library of Congress Cataloging-in-Publication Data
Names: Gish, Melissa, author.
Title: Dalai Lama / Melissa Gish.
Series: Odysseys in peace.
Includes bibliographical references and index.
Summary: A biography of Tibetan Buddhist leader Tenzin
Gyatso, examining his position as the 14th Dalai Lama and
his exile to India, as well as his emphasis on nonviolence and
other social stances.
Identifiers: ISBN 978-1-64026-162-4 (hardcover) / ISBN
978-1-62832-725-0 (pbk) / ISBN 978-1-64000-280-7
(eBook)
This title has been submitted for CIP processing under LCCN
2019935252.

First Edition HC 9 8 7 6 5 4 3 2 1
First Edition PBK 9 8 7 6 5 4 3 2 1

CONTENTS

Introduction

When the teachings of the **Buddha** first made their way into Tibet in the 4th century, Tibetan religion incorporated many aspects of Buddhist philosophy. Over the centuries, principles of Buddhism such as peace, compassion, and nonviolence became core values of Tibet's people. In the 15th century, Gedun Drupa, the 1st **Dalai Lama**, became the official spiritual leader of Tibet. Two hundred years later, the 5th Dalai Lama became also the temporal, or political, ruler of Tibet.

OPPOSITE: The title of lama is given to only a few dozen Tibetan Buddhist teachers who are revered for embodying the principles of Buddhism; the word *lama* means "wisdom."

Followers of Tibetan Buddhism believe in karma and reincarnation. A person who has achieved enlightenment may choose to end the cycle of reincarnation and find peace in nonexistence after death or be a *tulku*, one who is reborn in order to continue doing good for others. The Dalai Lama has chosen to be reincarnated 13 times. It is up to Tibetan Buddhist leaders to find each new Dalai Lama soon after birth. The current Dalai Lama, Tenzin Gyatso, was found as a toddler more than 80 years ago.

When China took control of Tibet in 1959, Tenzin Gyatso was forced to flee to India. Although he is no longer the political ruler of Tibet, he remains the spiritual leader of his homeland. He travels the world, exposing the plight of Tibetans under Chinese rule and promoting peace among all peoples. He is perhaps the most highly regarded spiritual leader in modern times, respected by people of all creeds who share his desire for peace and unity.

Finding the Dalai Lama

In far northeastern Tibet lies the region of Amdo. For centuries, **nomads** grazed their herds of yak and other animals there. In the early 20th century, Amdo was ruled by a **Muslim** warlord named Ma Pu-feng, who had established a regional government loyal to the Republic of China. In Amdo, about 20 families settled a tiny village they called Taktser. There, a man named

OPPOSITE: At Buddhist monasteries, large prayer wheels may be set in series stretching several miles; these wheels are always spun clockwise and are typically used during prayers to spread blessings and restore a positive karmic balance.

Choekyong Tsering, his wife Diki, and their children lived on a modest farm, growing potatoes, barley, and buckwheat. They also raised livestock such as horses and dzomo. The family's small, six-room house was made of stone and mud. It was in this house, on July 6, 1935, that a baby boy named Lhamo Thondup was born.

Lhamo Thondup's mother had been just 16 years old when she met Choekyong for the first time—at their wedding. The marriage had been arranged by their parents, as was customary then. Lhamo Thondup was Diki's fifth child. At

Choekyong Tsering was skilled with horses and had a reputation as a "healer of horses."

the time of Lhamo Thondup's birth, his eldest brother, Thubten Jigme Norbu, lived at Kumbum monastery, about 41 miles (66 km) away, where he was training to be a monk. Lhamo Thondup's next eldest brother, Gyalo Thondup, was also away at school in a neighboring village. A third brother, Lobsang Samten, was just three years old when his baby brother was born. The only girl, 18-year-old Tsering Dolma, helped Diki care for the little boys. Diki had 11 other children in her lifetime, but only 7 of her offspring would survive the hardship and illness that accompanied childhood in those days.

Choekyong Tsering was skilled with horses and had a reputation as a "healer of horses." Life in remote areas of Tibet involved bartering for goods rather than the use of currency. Choekyong raised and traded horses, along with other livestock, as a means of feeding and clothing his family. Choekyong's family practiced Tibetan Buddhism, and like his wife, Choekyong was a compassionate person who always helped others in need. Even during harsh times of drought and famine, strangers passing through Taktser could always find food and shelter at the Tsering farm.

For the first two years, Lhamo Thondup's life was quite ordinary, but then the weight of history descended upon him. When the 13th Dalai Lama, Thubten Gyatso, died in 1933, monks from Tibet's capital city of Lhasa were dispatched to search for his reincarnated being. Following clues that they believed were divine, they were led to the village of Taktser and to a two-year-old Lhamo Thondup, who seemed to recognize them. The

group pretended to be traders and visited with the people of the village. When they arrived at the Tsering farm, Lhamo Thondup greeted them with enthusiasm. The leader of the group, a monk named Kewtsang Rinpoche, asked Lhamo Thondup, "Do you know me?" The child replied, "Yes, Sera Lama." At this response, the monks took notice, for Rinpoche indeed was a lama from the Sera monastery. In fact, the child identified everyone in the search party.

The monks left to put a plan in order. A few days later, they returned to the Tsering farm. They showed Lhamo Thondup a number of artifacts—including a *mala* (string of prayer beads), bells, and even a teacup—that had belonged to Thubten Gyatso, along with some items that did not. The child immediately selected Thubten Gyatso's items and cried out, "It's mine! It's mine!"

Though this evidence was compelling, the monks needed more proof. They asked many more questions and challenged Lhamo Thondup to more tests. Before long, however, they determined that this child was, indeed, the reincarnation of Thubten Gyatso. The monks had undoubtedly found the 14th Dalai Lama. The monks prepared to take the new Dalai Lama and his family to Lhasa, but their excitement was short-lived, for their discovery of him led to political conflict in Amdo.

When Ma Pu-feng learned that the 14th Dalai Lama had been discovered in his territory, he thought he could use the situation to earn favor with political leaders in China. He would not allow the monks to take the boy to Lhasa without a Chinese army escort. This would effectively put the boy—and the whole of Tibet—under Chinese control. When the monks refused, Ma Pu-feng

Ma Pu-feng ... insisted on a payment of silver valued at 100,000 Chinese dollars in exchange for the boy's freedom to travel unescorted.

then insisted on a payment of silver valued at 100,000 Chinese dollars in exchange for the boy's freedom to travel unescorted. The ransom was paid, and the monks took the boy to Kumbum monastery, where a ceremony took place to introduce him as the 14th Dalai Lama. The monks were just about to continue their journey to Lhasa with Lhamo Thondup when Ma Pu-feng made another demand. This time he would not allow the monks to leave Kumbum unless they paid him 330,000 dollars. The monks sought the advice of the Tibetan government, which refused to allow the Chinese government to control the Dalai Lama's fate. Negotiations dragged on for two years, but the Tibetans, with the help of the Indian government, raised enough money to satisfy Ma Pu-feng.

Now four years old, the Dalai Lama arrived at his destination on October 8, 1939. Near the city gates of Lhasa, a group of tents had been erected. In the center of the encampment, a huge blue-and-white tent held an ornately carved wooden throne. During a daylong ceremony, Lhamo Thondup was introduced to the people. Crowds of people gathered to glimpse the boy who would, at the proper age, assume the responsibilities

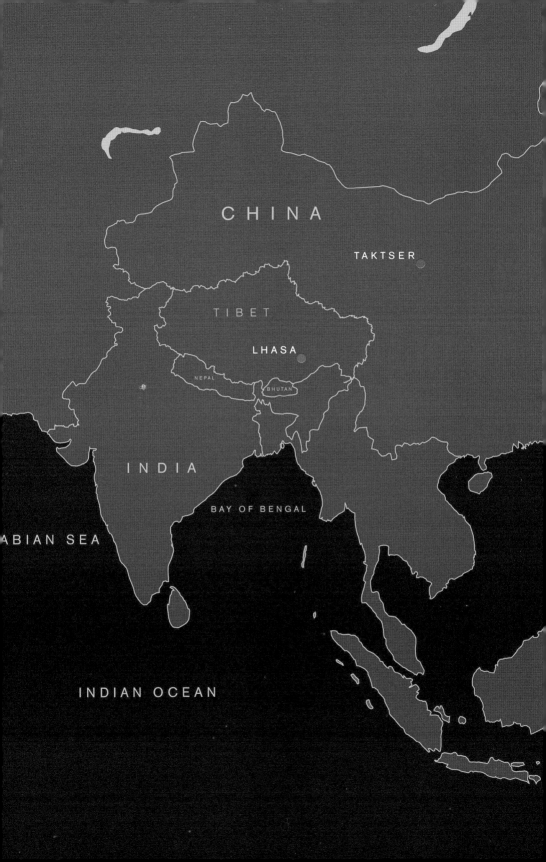

that went along with his new title. After the ceremony, Lhamo Thondup and his brother Lobsang Samten were taken to Norbulingka Palace, a monastery just west of Lhasa. The boys lived there for one year, playing happily together and visiting with their parents often. Then, at age five, Lhamo Thondup was taken to nearby Potala Palace, a massive, 13-story monastery built high on a mountain. There, in another ceremony—this one grander than the previous—he was officially installed as the spiritual leader of Tibet. At Potala, he also began his monastic training—training that would shape the rest of his life as the 14th Dalai Lama.

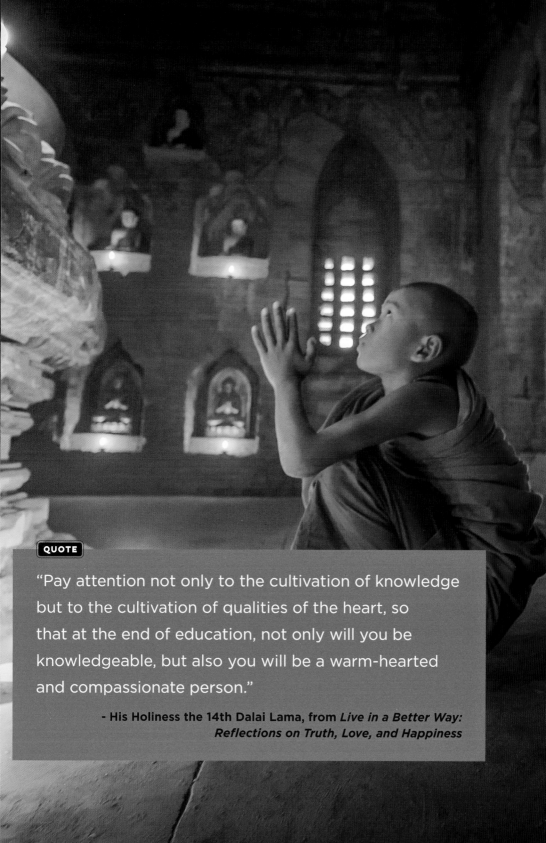

"Pay attention not only to the cultivation of knowledge but to the cultivation of qualities of the heart, so that at the end of education, not only will you be knowledgeable, but also you will be a warm-hearted and compassionate person."

- His Holiness the 14th Dalai Lama, from *Live in a Better Way: Reflections on Truth, Love, and Happiness*

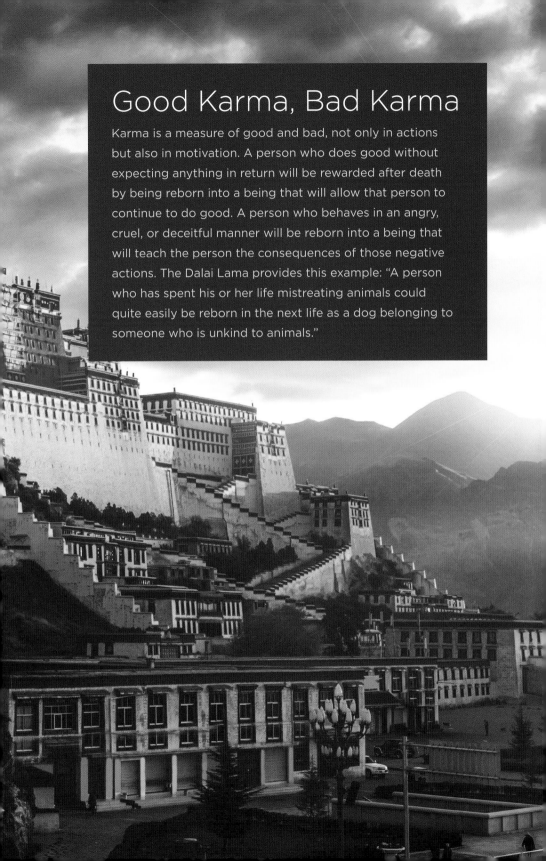

Good Karma, Bad Karma

Karma is a measure of good and bad, not only in actions but also in motivation. A person who does good without expecting anything in return will be rewarded after death by being reborn into a being that will allow that person to continue to do good. A person who behaves in an angry, cruel, or deceitful manner will be reborn into a being that will teach the person the consequences of those negative actions. The Dalai Lama provides this example: "A person who has spent his or her life mistreating animals could quite easily be reborn in the next life as a dog belonging to someone who is unkind to animals."

Becoming the Dalai Lama

As a new student, the Dalai Lama was taken to Jokhang Temple, located within Lhasa, where, in a traditional ritual, his head was shaved, and he was dressed in the maroon-colored robes of a novice monk. Back at Potala Palace, the Dalai Lama's initial education consisted of learning to read. His brother Lobsang Samten was schooled with him. Having no other playmates, the boys sought

OPPOSITE: Known for their detailed and intricate architecture, elaborate Tibetan-inspired buildings found across Central Asia draw thousands of tourists each year.

companionship with the cleaning staff, who happily played with them. The young Dalai Lama particularly enjoyed skating across the palace's freshly polished stone floors and secretly exploring the palace, for Potala contained more than 1,000 rooms!

When the Dalai Lama was eight years old, his brother was sent to a different monastery. Now there were no distractions from his studies. However, the young Dalai Lama was saddened and lonely. His mother and sister were allowed to visit occasionally. When he grew a little older, his mother also brought a new baby brother, Tenzin Choegyal, to visit. For the most part, though, Lhamo Thondup was isolated. He became so lonely that he began encouraging mice to live in his cold, dreary bedroom, so he could watch their antics at night.

Guardian Bird

The night after the birth of the 1st Dalai Lama, bandits raided the house, chasing his parents away without him. The next day, his frantic parents returned to find their baby perfectly safe, guarded by a huge crow. When the 1st Dalai Lama grew up, he reached out through meditation and contacted the spirit of that crow. A protective deity, or god, called Mahakala told him that he would always watch out for him in the body of a crow. Later, crows also resided at the homes of the 7th, 8th, 12th, and 14th Dalai Lamas. The current Dalai Lama believes Mahakala, crows, and the Dalai

Lhamo Thondup's life as a novice monk was strictly scheduled for him. He awoke at dawn and prayed and meditated for an hour before starting his day. He had lessons in Buddhist scripture, calligraphy, logic, art, music, drama, and poetry, as well as medicine, astrology, language, and Tibetan culture. He also learned and practiced the art of debate, a vital skill for a political leader of Tibet. He was allowed some playtime and had an extensive collection of toys—gifts from followers around the world. For years, Lhamo Thondup's daily routine was the same. Only his location varied, with winters spent at Potala Palace and summers at Norbulingka Palace.

The Dalai Lama soon discovered an interest in mechanics and technology. Among the 13th Dalai Lama's artifacts kept at the palaces were a telescope, a clock

This fascination with technology would continue to grow, eventually leading the Dalai Lama to promote a relationship between Buddhism and science.

with a rotating globe that showed the time in different time zones, and a film projector. As World War II raged around the world, newsreels made their way to Tibet through India, giving the Dalai Lama his first glimpses of war, and a collection of Charlie Chaplin's silent films sparked in the Dalai Lama a love of movies that would remain for the rest of his life. The 13th Dalai Lama also left three cars, whose engines the young Dalai Lama learned to repair. This fascination with technology would continue to grow, eventually leading the Dalai Lama to promote a relationship between Buddhism and science.

When he was 14 years old, the Dalai Lama traveled to the Drepung monastery, near Lhasa, to debate his interpretations of the Buddhist religion with the high lamas there. This would be a test of his educational preparation as well as his ability to speak publically. Thousands of monks gathered to hear the debates. Austrian explorer and writer Heinrich Harrer was also there. He reported that the Dalai Lama was "never for a moment disconcerted," while his opponent "was hard put to hold his own." Harrer became a trusted friend of the Dalai Lama and tutored him in science and technology, including the workings of jet engines.

As a young man, the Dalai Lama had to mature quickly. A civil war in China meant trouble for Tibet. Chinese forces wanted troops and resources from Tibet. The 15-year-old Dalai Lama assumed full political

Learn from Buddhism

The Dalai Lama recognizes that Buddhist scripture or even meditation is not for everyone. But he believes the principles of Buddhism can be useful to anyone and emphasizes Buddha's philosophy of **cultural relativism**. Kathleen Norris, in *Amazing Grace: A Vocabulary of Faith,* recounts a time when a reporter asked the Dalai Lama what he would say to Americans who want to become Buddhists. "Don't bother," the Dalai Lama said. "Learn from Buddhism, if that is good for you. But do it as a Christian, a Jew, or whatever you are. And be a good friend to us."

power in November 1950, ready to negotiate with the Chinese. But there was no negotiating with China's new leader, Chairman Mao Tse-tung. Under threat of full-scale invasion, the Dalai Lama was soon forced to sign the Seventeen Point Agreement that would allow China to recruit Tibetan citizens for its armed forces and require Tibet to defend China against its enemies. The Tibetan army's 8,500 men stood no chance against the 80,000 Chinese troops poised to invade Tibet. The Dalai Lama saw the agreement as the only way to avoid the destruction of his country.

In an effort to calm relations between China and Tibet, the Dalai Lama visited Chairman Mao in China. The Dalai Lama spent six months in Beijing, the first major city he had ever seen. He toured schools, hospitals, hydroelectric plants, and factories. He saw paved roads and vehicles everywhere. Chairman Mao wanted Tibet to become part of China and tried to coax the Dalai Lama's compliance by offering to deliver such modernization to Tibet. "Tibet is a great country," Chairman Mao told him at one of their meetings. "Long ago you even conquered a lot of China. But now you have fallen behind and we want to help you." The Dalai Lama listened to Mao's proposal with suspicion, for he had learned of Chairman Mao's anti-religious viewpoint. When Chairman Mao told him, "Religion is poison … it neglects material progress," the Dalai Lama knew that Chinese involvement in Tibet would be disastrous. He thought to himself, "So, you are the destroyer of the Dharma after all." He tried to explain that Tibetans were a religious people who felt that their inner peace was more important than material goods. He told Chairman Mao, "China and Tibet are

When Chairman Mao told him, "Religion is poison … it neglects material progress," the Dalai Lama knew that Chinese involvement in Tibet would be disastrous.

like fire and wood."

Nevertheless, in a bid to slowly take over Tibet, the Chinese began improving roads and bridges. They also built schools and hospitals in Tibet. Yet they simultaneously took steps to dismantle Buddhist religion and influence Tibetan culture. Monasteries were destroyed, and monks were murdered. The people rebelled against the intruders—often at the cost of their own lives. The Dalai Lama tried to negotiate peace and asked other nations, including the United States, for assistance. No one would help Tibet. By 1958, Chairman Mao just wanted to end the conflict quickly—he would capture the Dalai Lama and force him to surrender Tibet. In early 1959, he ordered the Dalai Lama to appear, alone, at the Chinese headquarters. Word of the trap spread like wildfire. Thousands of Tibetans took to the streets to prevent the Dalai Lama's capture and to demand an end to Chinese interference in their country. The buildup of Chinese troops continued, and the call went out to locate the Dalai Lama. The 23-year-old Dalai Lama knew he could not serve his people if he was dead. Anticipating his assassination, he had no other choice but to flee his homeland. On March 17, 1959, he and his family left Tibet.

"With inner strength, we can face problems on the familial, societal, and even global levels in a more realistic way. Nonviolence does not mean passivity. We need to solve problems through dialogue in a spirit of reconciliation. This is the real meaning of nonviolence and the source of world peace."

- His Holiness the 14th Dalai Lama, from *Illuminating the Path to Enlightenment*

Leading in Exile

Tens of thousands of Chinese troops had amassed in and around Lhasa—every one of them on the lookout for the Dalai Lama. Thousands of Tibetan demonstrators had also gathered around Norbulingka Palace in an effort to protect their beloved Dalai Lama. It was late at night. The Dalai Lama donned a pair of trousers and a long, black coat. He slung a rifle over his shoulder and tucked his glasses into his pocket. Only a handful of soldiers

OPPOSITE: Lhasa's sprawling Potala Palace so impressed the Chinese premier that he sent his own troops to protect the structure, sparing it from the destructive Cultural Revolution.

knew of his escape plan. Chikya Kenpo, a trusted security guard armed with a sword, told the Dalai Lama, "Stay by me at all costs." They left the palace, the Dalai Lama's heart pounding. He knew his capture would spell the end for his people. Chinese spies had infiltrated the demonstrators, and no one could be trusted. Stepping into the crowd, the soldiers announced that they were heading out to patrol the area. The Dalai Lama kept his face down. Without his glasses, he could barely see. Finally, they were free of the palace grounds and heading toward the Kyichu River.

They quietly rowed a small boat across the river, careful to avoid the Chinese patrols. On the other side, the Dalai Lama's mother, brother, sister, and two of his teachers were waiting. Earlier that night, a party of freedom fighters had helped them escape Lhasa and

Nearly 800 artillery shells were fired into Norbulingka, and 2,000 people were tortured and murdered.

brought ponies and mules for the journey. Joined by some Buddhist officials and trusted advisers, the Dalai Lama's party headed south. As he traveled, the Dalai Lama thought about how he would negotiate with China's leaders. Then, on the fifth day of the journey, a messenger brought terrible news. Word of his escape had reached Chinese officials, and two days after he had left Lhasa, the full force of the Chinese army was unleashed. Nearly 800 artillery shells were fired into Norbulingka, and 2,000 people were tortured and murdered. Mao Tse-tung dissolved the Tibetan government and put Tibet under the control of the People's Republic of China. The Dalai Lama later wrote that he realized with this news "that it would be impossible to negotiate with people who behaved in this cruel and criminal fashion."

He returned word that the Chinese attack invalidated the Seventeen Point Agreement, and he held that the Tibetan government was free and independent. He wanted his people to know that he would still stand up for them. Then his party continued toward India. For nine more days, they struggled over the Himalayas, trekking through three-mile-high (4.8 km) mountain passes and braving roaring blizzards. They managed to evade the Chinese forces in pursuit. The Dalai Lama was struck with dysentery and developed a fever. He became too weak to ride a pony. Near the end of the journey, a villager gave the Dalai Lama a dzomo, on whose broad back he

could safely be carried. The party finally reached the Indian border two weeks after their daring escape from Lhasa. The Dalai Lama later wrote, "Only the thought of my responsibility to the six million Tibetans kept me going. That and my faith."

India's prime minister Jawaharlal Nehru welcomed the Dalai Lama and granted him and his party asylum. India was no friend to China. At a press briefing on April 4, 1959, Nehru said, "That a deeply spiritual and temporal ruler of a peaceful nation should have been forced to flee his country is a powerful indictment of Communist China's policy toward Tibet." While the Dalai Lama worked with political leaders in India to help urge an end to the violence in Tibet, his people began fleeing the country. Tens of thousands of refugees poured into neighboring Bhutan, Nepal, and India. Students and young orphans were taken in by various European nations, and programs were organized to help people establish new homes in India. Many countries, including the U.S. and Canada, participated in relief efforts.

In 1960, the Dalai Lama and other Tibetan political leaders established the Tibetan Kashag Government, later renamed the Central Tibetan Administration (CTA) and also referred to as the Tibetan Government in Exile. Nehru allowed the Tibetans to headquarter this entity in the city of Dharamshala, where it still exists today. The CTA is tasked with running schools and healthcare facilities and funding cultural activities and economic development programs for Tibetans living in India. It also aids the more than 1,000 Tibetan refugees who continue to enter India each year.

During his first years in India, the Dalai Lama learned

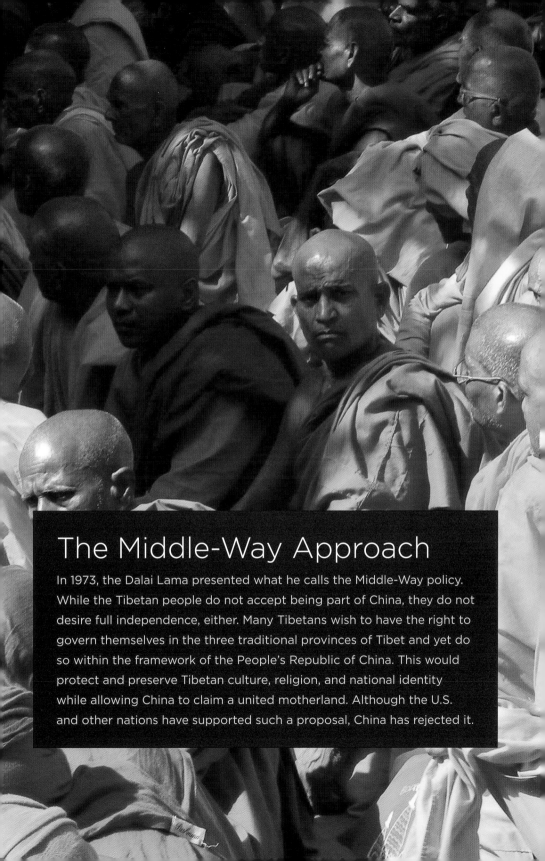

The Middle-Way Approach

In 1973, the Dalai Lama presented what he calls the Middle-Way policy. While the Tibetan people do not accept being part of China, they do not desire full independence, either. Many Tibetans wish to have the right to govern themselves in the three traditional provinces of Tibet and yet do so within the framework of the People's Republic of China. This would protect and preserve Tibetan culture, religion, and national identity while allowing China to claim a united motherland. Although the U.S. and other nations have supported such a proposal, China has rejected it.

English. To deal with the stress of his political responsibilities, he relied on meditation and a renewed study of Buddha's teachings. He also resumed his old interest in watch repair, and he filled his house with dogs and cats, which allowed him to practice compassion for animals. People from around the world began to visit him, eager to hear his story and learn how they could help Tibet in its struggle for freedom. Soon, the Dalai Lama began to receive invitations to visit other countries. He embarked on his first journey outside India in 1967, when he went to Japan and Thailand. In 1973, he made his first trip to Europe and Scandinavia, visiting 11 countries over a period of 6 weeks. In Rome, he met Pope Paul VI. In Switzerland, he met 200 Tibetan children who had been adopted into Swiss families. In Scandinavia, he visited the organizations that helped young Tibetan men and women train as mechanics and agriculturalists. His first trip to the U.S. took place in 1979.

nvitations to travel abroad began to involve requests for the Dalai Lama to address groups of people. Over the years, the Dalai Lama has spoken countless times about his three main principles. First, he explains "universal responsibility," referring to the responsibility that humans have for each other, for all sentient beings, and for all of nature. This doctrine promotes compassion, forgiveness, tolerance, contentment, and self-discipline. Secondly, he encourages people to seek harmony and understanding among different religions. It is his firm belief that "all religions aim at making people better human beings, and despite philosophical differences, they all aim at helping humanity to find happiness." Thirdly, he talks about his own country and people with the goals of keeping Tibetan language and culture alive and of encouraging the protection of Tibet's natural environment. For Tibetans in exile, the Dalai Lama explained, "our priority must be resettlement and the continuity of our cultural traditions. As to the future, with Truth, Justice, and Courage as our weapons, we Tibetans would eventually prevail in regaining freedom for Tibet."

"My being a Buddhist monk does not mean I believe that it is only by practicing Buddhism that people can bring happiness to themselves and others. On the contrary, I believe that this is possible even for people who have no religion at all."

– His Holiness the 14th Dalai Lama, from *Freedom in Exile*

A Voice for Peace

For 20 years, China kept its treatment of Tibet a secret from the world, closing its borders and **censoring** journalists. In 1978, the newly elected president of the People's Republic of China, Chiang Ching-kuo, wanted to demonstrate that China's control of Tibet had been positive. He claimed publically that Chinese and Tibetan people lived together in peace and that everyone was happy. The Dalai Lama wanted to believe Chiang, who,

OPPOSITE: Exiled Tibetans and supporters gather annually on March 10 to commemorate the day Tibetans enabled the Dalai Lama's escape, which has since become known as Tibetan Uprising Day.

in 1979, allowed the Dalai Lama to send five dignitaries to Tibet to see for themselves. Their reports did not corroborate Chiang's story, though.

I t came to light that the Chinese used forced Tibetan labor to build and run power plants, factories, and large-scale agricultural operations. Tibet's natural resources such as its forests and minerals were being exploited, and large-scale livestock farming had replaced the wilderness, extirpating native wildlife and leaving entire ecosystems devastated. Almost all the goods produced in Tibet went to China, leaving the Tibetan people without adequate food or resources. Also, nuclear weapons were being manufactured and stored in Tibet, and nuclear waste was being dumped there.

The Dalai Lama later wrote of the "years of famine, mass starvation, public execution, and gross and disgusting violations of human rights, not the least of which included the abduction of children either into forced labor gangs or for 'education' in China, the imprisonment of innocent citizens, and the deaths of thousands of monks and nuns in concentration camps." In addition, Tibetans are not allowed to practice Buddhism. The Dalai Lama's picture is banned, and followers are arrested for celebrating his birthday. Anyone who protests against China is imprisoned and tortured, and Tibetans attempting to flee the country are killed.

China has continued to deny all allegations of wrongdoing in Tibet, and official statements from the Chinese government have called the Dalai Lama "a terrorist," "a wolf wrapped in a monk's robe," and "a demon." Yunliang Zhou, a spokesperson for the Chinese consulate in San Francisco, once told a reporter, "The words and deeds of the Dalai Lama over past decades are self-evident that he's not just a religious figure but a political exile bent on separatist activities under the disguise of religion."

In fact, the Dalai Lama does not favor severing ties between Tibet and China. In the 1970s, his call for independence changed to one for restored religious freedom and cultural protection. As the Dalai Lama's message spread around the world in the 1980s, numerous organizations formed to support Tibet's interests. Groups such as Free Tibet, the International Campaign for Tibet, and Students for a Free Tibet emerged to use education and

Censorship in Tibet

The emergence of social media and online news makes it easier for people to communicate—except in Tibet, where the Chinese government has imposed blocks on many Internet sites. In addition, electronic identification (eID) chips are embedded in cell phones, allowing the government to listen to conversations and read text messages. This is because the Chinese government wishes to control what people see, hear, and say about Tibet. The human rights group International Campaign for Tibet was told by a Tibetan now in exile, "Now many of us have simply stopped speaking to family and friends inside Tibet, because of the dangers. It is as if the Communist Party can reach inside our minds now."

Five-Point Peace Plan

On September 21, 1987, the Dalai Lama spoke to the U.S. Congressional Human Rights Caucus in Washington, D.C., and presented a five-part plan to restore peace and human rights in Tibet with the following goals:

1. The establishment of a "zone of peace" throughout Tibet.
2. Abandonment of China's "population transfer policy" of bringing Chinese into Tibet to make Tibetans the minority.
3. Respect for Tibetans' human rights and democratic freedoms.
4. Environmental protection and the cessation of nuclear-waste dumping.
5. Begin to talk about repairing the relationship between Tibetans and Chinese.

While the rest of the world applauded this proposal for peace, China denounced the plan.

nonviolent activism to advocate for the Tibetan people. One strategy that some groups have encouraged is an economic boycott of China. But the Dalai Lama believes this would unfairly burden everyday Chinese people. Instead, he promotes diplomacy based on friendship.

The Dalai Lama has received numerous awards and distinctions. For his efforts toward a peaceful compromise with China, he was awarded the Nobel Peace Prize in 1989. In 2007, president George W. Bush was authorized by Congress to present the Dalai Lama with the

At the age of 76, the Dalai Lama retired as the political leader of the CTA.

U.S. Congressional Gold Medal. "We honor him as a universal symbol of peace and tolerance, a shepherd for the faithful, and the keeper of the flame for his people," Bush said. In 2012, Dr. John M. Templeton awarded the Dalai Lama the Templeton Prize, noting, "He has encouraged serious scientific investigative review of the power of compassion and its potential to address fundamental problems of the world."

At the age of 76, the Dalai Lama retired as the political leader of the CTA. The democratically elected *sikyong*, or president, Lobsang Sangay took on the mantle and won re-election in 2016. In an interview with the *New York Times*, Sangay said that he would seek the

U.S. Shows Support

In July 1985, Tibet received its first official political support. Ninety-one members of the U.S. Congress signed a letter to the president of the People's Republic of China, Li Xiannian, urging talks between the Chinese government and representatives of the Dalai Lama. U.S. support continued into the next decade. In a 1992 letter to the Dalai Lama, president George H. W. Bush wrote that the U.S. was "urging the Chinese to use the vehicle of dialogue constructively to ease tension and work toward peaceful results." In 2002, the U.S. passed the Tibetan Policy Act "to support the aspirations of the Tibetan people to safeguard their distinct identity." Today, the U.S. continues to encourage peace talks between Chinese and Tibetan leaders.

One topic that the Dalai Lama says is most urgent is climate change. His interest in science has led him to discuss our planet's fate with scientists and experts from around the world.

support of other nations in pressuring China to at least listen to the Dalai Lama's concerns about his people. He also stated that he would focus on "improving educational opportunities for Tibetan exiles and improving their economic opportunities."

Owing to his advanced age, the Dalai Lama travels less and has appointed emissaries to speak on his behalf. He welcomes visitors to his home in Dharamshala, India, where he is happy to give interviews. One topic that the Dalai Lama says is most urgent is climate change. His interest in science has led him to discuss our planet's fate with scientists and experts from around the world. In speaking about climate change, the Dalai Lama has said, "This is not a question of one nation or two nations. This is a question of humanity. Our world is our home. There's no other planet where we may move or shift." The Dalai Lama is also concerned about military build-ups and nuclear weapons. In Japan, speaking at a 2018 event focusing on the relationship of modern science and Buddhism, the Dalai Lama explained that "the use of violence is out of date. Peace in the world won't be achieved unless people develop inner peace. The goal of a demilitarized world will not be achieved until individuals start to implement inner disarmament."

Over the decades, the Dalai Lama has met with many world leaders, including four U.S. presidents.

Universal Responsibility

In a 2008 talk in London, the Dalai Lama explained how Buddhists "consider all sentient beings as the mother sentient being, to whom you should develop the same sense of closeness as to your own mother." He likened this to other religions, such as Christianity and Islam, which hold that "all creation is created by God.... and [Muslims believe] a true Muslim should love the whole of creation as much as they love God. So different words, a different approach, but the same meaning. Therefore, there is the idea that there is a sense of global responsibility, that we should develop a sense of concern for the whole of humanity, the whole world."

He has inspired countless people to seek peace among individuals, communities, and entire nations. When he dies, his loss will be felt by millions, particularly because he may be the last Dalai Lama. "The very purpose of a reincarnation," he has said, "is to continue the unfinished work of the previous incarnation." The Dalai Lama believes he has done good work and therefore may choose to end the cycle of reincarnation. Whether this happens remains to be seen, for the Dalai Lama has said that if he reincarnates, it will be in a being born outside of Tibet and China, and it will be up to Tibetan monks to locate this person. Regardless of what the future holds, many people will remember this Dalai Lama as one of history's most respected and beloved seekers of peace.

"Now in the 21st century we have the chance to create a better situation. Problems won't disappear; they may increase, but adopting a peaceful approach means that we will address them by nonviolent means. We need the confidence that comes from having truth on your side; it is powerful support."

- His Holiness the 14th Dalai Lama, in a 2013 speech at the University of Cambridge

Timeline

1933   On December 17, the 13th Dalai Lama (Thubten Gyatso) dies in Lhasa, Tibet, at age 57.

1935   Lhamo Thondup, believed to be the reincarnation of Thubten Gyatso, is born in Taktser, Tibet, on July 6.

1939   Arriving in Lhasa on October 8 after a 10-week journey, Lhamo Thondup is officially recognized as the 14th Dalai Lama and given the monastic name Tenzin Gyatso.

1940   After the Official Enthronement Ceremony, Tenzin Gyatso begins monastic education on February 22.

1950   Eighty thousand Chinese soldiers invade Tibet on November 17; the Dalai Lama assumes full political power.

1951   Pressured by China, the Tibetan government signs the Seventeen Point Agreement for the Peaceful Liberation of Tibet on May 23, affirming China's sovereignty over Tibet.

1954   Beginning in July, the Dalai Lama engages in peace talks with Chairman Mao Tse-tung and other Chinese leaders for almost a year.

1959   On March 17, the Dalai Lama makes a nighttime escape from the artillery bombardment of Norbulingka Palace.

1973   From September to November, the Dalai Lama travels to Europe to raise awareness of Tibet's plight and promote world peace.

1987   The Dalai Lama delivers his Five-Point Peace Plan for Tibet to members of the U.S. Congress on September 21.

1989　The Dalai Lama is awarded the Nobel Peace Prize in Oslo, Norway.

2011　In May, the Dalai Lama transfers official political power to the democratically elected leader of Tibet, Lobsang Sangay, ending a 368-year-old tradition.

2018　Tibetan Buddhist leaders meet in India in November to discuss the choosing of the 14th Dalai Lama's successor.

Selected Bibliography

Dalai Lama. *My Spiritual Journey.* Trans. Charlotte Mandell. New York: HarperLuxe, 2010.

Dalai Lama, and Franz Alt. *An Appeal to the World: The Way to Peace in a Time of Division.* New York: William Morrow, 2017.

Dalai Lama, and Sofia Stril-Rever. *A Call for Revolution: A Vision for the Future.* New York: William Morrow, 2017.

Lama Tsomo. *Why is the Dalai Lama Always Smiling?: A Westerner's Introduction and Guide to Tibetan Buddhist Practices.* Missoula, Mont.: Namchak, 2016.

Meachen Ran, Dana. *Who is the Dalai Lama?* New York: Penguin Workshop, 2018.

Nagle, Jeanne. Dalai Lama: *Spiritual Leader of the Tibetan People.* New York: Britannica, 2015.

Rai, Raghu. *A God in Exile: The Fourteenth Dalai Lama.* New Delhi: Roli Books, 2018.

Schwieger, Peter. *The Dalai Lama and the Emperor of China: A Political History of the Tibetan Institution of Reincarnation.* New York: Columbia University Press, 2015.

Endnotes

asylum
protection granted by a nation to someone who has left his or her native country because of religious or political persecution

Buddha
also known as Siddhartha Gautama, an Indian spiritual leader who lived 2,500 years ago and on whose teachings the philosophy and religion of Buddhism are founded

calligraphy
artistic handwriting featuring flourishes or ornaments

censoring
suppressing part or all of a communication (such as a news report, book, movie, or piece of art)

cultural relativism
the concept that people's beliefs, values, and behaviors should be understood on the basis of their own history and culture and not judged against other cultures'

Dalai Lama
the spiritual leader of Tibetan Buddhism and, until the establishment of Chinese rule over Tibet, the political leader of Tibet

Dharma
an understanding and acceptance of Buddha's teachings, which are called the *Dhamma*, meaning "truth"

dysentery
an infection of the intestines resulting in severe diarrhea and abdominal pain; caused by bacteria, viruses, or parasites

dzomo	Tibetan name for a female offspring of crossbred cattle and yak; a male is called a dzo
enlightenment	in Buddhism, a state of supreme knowledge of truth and compassion that leads to an end of suffering; also known as Nirvana
Jawaharlal Nehru	the first prime minister of India from its establishment as an independent nation in 1947 until his death in 1964; he was a scholar of Buddhist scriptures
karma	in Buddhism, a person's motivations and actions in this and previous lives, which decide his or her fate in future lives
Mao Tse-tung	also known as Mao Zedong; Chinese politician who founded the People's Republic of China in 1949 after 20 years of civil war and ruled until his death in 1976
monk	member of a religious community of men typically living under established vows based on humility; female monks are called nuns
Muslim	of or pertaining to the religion, law, or civilization of Islam, which has the Koran as its sacred scripture and teaches that there is only one God and that Muhammad is his prophet
nomads	people with no fixed home who move, often according to the seasons, in search of food, water, or grazing land
reincarnation	the rebirth of a soul in a new body

sentient	possessing the capability to perceive experiences through the senses of touch, taste, sight, hearing, or smell
separatist	providing support for the separation of a particular group of people from a larger body, especially on the basis of ethnicity, religion, or gender

Websites

Free Tibet
https://freetibet.org/about

Learn about Tibet's history, culture, and religion, including Tibetan resistance to China's occupation and control.

His Holiness the 14th Dalai Lama of Tibet
https://www.dalailama.com/

Learn more about the 14th Dalai Lama's life, mission, and legacy through interviews, stories, pictures, videos, and the Dalai Lama's own words.

Note: Every effort has been made to ensure that any websites listed above were active at the time of publication. However, because of the nature of the Internet, it is impossible to guarantee that these sites will remain active indefinitely or that their contents will not be altered.

Index